Smithsonian

THOMAS JEFFERSON'S WRITING DESK

What an Artifact Can Tell Us About the Declaration of Independence

by John Micklos Jr.

CAPSTONE PRESS
a capstone imprint

Capstone Captivate is published by Capstone Press,
an imprint of Capstone.
1710 Roe Crest Drive
North Mankato, Minnesota 56003
www.capstonepub.com

Library of Congress Cataloging-in-Publication Data is available on the Library of Congress website.

ISBN: 978-1-4966-9576-5 (library binding)
ISBN: 978-1-4966-9686-1 (paperback)
ISBN: 978-1-9771-5514-6 (ebook pdf)

Summary: With the Declaration of Independence, the 13 American colonies demanded independence from Great Britain. Thomas Jefferson was chosen to write it. But did he write every word? Who helped him? Discover the answers and learn about the desk Jefferson designed and at which he wrote this important document.

Image Credits
Architect of the Capitol: 30; Bridgeman Images: Wood Ronsaville Harlin, Inc. USA, 5 (top); Dreamstime: Joe Sohm, 40; Getty Images: The LIFE Picture Collection/Alfred Eisenstaedt, 10; iStockphoto: ilbusca, 32; Library of Congress: cover (back), 5 (bottom), 22, 24, 27, 31, 35, 37 (top); Line of Battle Enterprise: 6, 33; The Metropolitan Museum of Art: Purchase, Sansbury-Mills and Rogers Funds, Emily Crane Chadbourne Gift, Virginia Groomes Gift, in memory of Mary W. Groomes, Mr. and Mrs. Marshall P. Blankarn, John Bierwirth and Robert G. Goelet Gifts, The Sylmaris Collection, Gift of George Coe Graves, by exchange, Gift of Mrs. Russell Sage, by exchange, and funds from various donors, 1974, 15; National Archives and Records Administration: cover background and throughout; National Park Service: Independence National Historical Park, 45; Newscom: Everett Collection, 11, Heritage Images/English Heritage, 18; North Wind Picture Archives: 16, 21, 23, 37 (bottom); Shutterstock: Adam Parent, 43, Everett Collection, 26, Inspired By Maps, 44; Smithsonian Institution: National Museum of American History, cover (bottom left), 1, 8, 13, 14, 42, National Portrait Gallery, 34, Smithsonian American Art Museum, Transfer from the Archives of American Art, 28; Wikimedia: Library of Congress/University of Virginia Library, Special Collections Department, University Archives, Thomas Jefferson Architectural Drawings, 38, William Morris, 39; XNR Productions: 7, 19

Editorial Credits
Editor: Michelle Bisson; Designer: Tracy Davies; Media Researcher: Svetlana Zhurkin; Production Specialist: Tori Abraham

Smithsonian Credits
Barbara Clark Smith, Museum Curator, Division of Political, National Museum of American History; Bethanee Bemis, Museum Specialist, Division of Political History, National Museum of American History

All internet sites appearing in back matter were available and accurate when this book was sent to press.

TABLE OF CONTENTS

Words in **bold** are in the glossary.

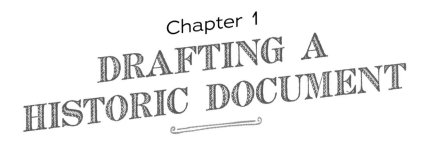

Chapter 1
DRAFTING A HISTORIC DOCUMENT

Thomas Jefferson hunched over his small wooden writing desk. He opened the desk drawer. He pulled out a quill pen and some paper. He thought for a moment and dipped his pen into the glass inkwell sitting on the desk. Then he wrote down some words. It was late June 1776 in Philadelphia, Pennsylvania. His rented rooms on the second story of Jacob Graff's house were hot and stuffy. Sometimes he had to swat away horseflies.

Jefferson had been working on the same document for about two weeks. Progress was slow. Each day, he walked a few blocks to the Pennsylvania State House. There, he met with other **delegates** to the Second Continental Congress. These delegates came from each of the 13 American colonies. They were making a hard decision. Should they break away from Great Britain and form a new country? Jefferson split his time between working with Congress and writing.

Thomas Jefferson worked day and night on what would become one of the most important documents in U.S. history.

Continental Congress

The Continental Congress was the governing body for the colonies. The First Continental Congress met in Philadelphia in 1774. Philadelphia was the largest city in the colonies. It was also centrally located. That made it easier for delegates to travel

The Continental Congress met in the State House in Philadelphia.

there. This Congress tried to mend ties with Great Britain. The Second Continental Congress met in Philadelphia from 1775 to 1781. By 1775, the Revolutionary War (1775–1783) had started. This Congress declared independence from Great Britain. It led the war effort for the new United States.

In 1776, more than 2 million people lived in the 13 American colonies. The colonists were British **subjects**. This meant they were ruled by George III, the king of Great Britain. For many years, the system worked well. But over time, things changed. The colonists grew angry over being taxed by British **Parliament**, among other things. They were upset that they had no voice in the British government. They argued that only their own elected colonial legislatures could tax them. Tensions between the British government and the colonists grew worse.

The Battles of Lexington and Concord marked the start of the Revolutionary War.

In April 1775, battles broke out between colonists and British soldiers near Boston, Massachusetts. This marked the beginning of the Revolutionary War. By mid-1776, many colonists believed it was time to break away from Great Britain. They thought the colonies should form a new nation. Colonial leaders asked Thomas Jefferson of Virginia—a skilled writer—to draft a statement. This statement would explain why this drastic step was needed.

Chapter 2

A SPECIAL PAPER, A SPECIAL DESK

The document that Jefferson wrote was only about 1,800 words. That's about half the length of this book. But he spent more than two weeks working on it. He wanted to make every word just right. In the paper, he explained that the colonists were fighting for basic human rights. These rights included "Life, Liberty, and the pursuit of Happiness." Then Jefferson listed the reasons why the colonies were breaking away from Great Britain.

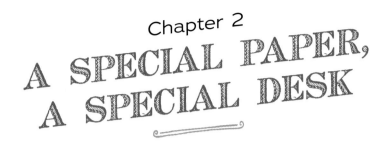

Thomas Jefferson himself designed the portable desk on which he wrote the Declaration of Independence and many other important papers.

Jefferson wrote his statement on a simple wooden writing desk. He had designed the desk himself. He hired a skilled woodworker to build it. Jefferson used the desk for more than 50 years. He wrote many important letters and papers on it. The one he wrote in 1776 was the most famous of them all. It became known as the **Declaration** of Independence. It ranks among the world's most famous documents. Because of this, the desk has become an important **artifact** of American history.

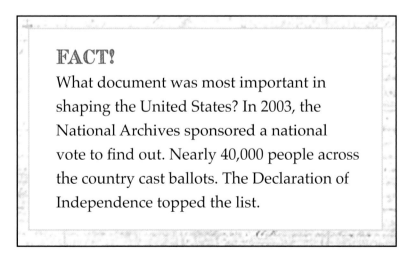

FACT!

What document was most important in shaping the United States? In 2003, the National Archives sponsored a national vote to find out. Nearly 40,000 people across the country cast ballots. The Declaration of Independence topped the list.

Thomas Jefferson loved to design things. His home, called Monticello, in Virginia featured many of his creations. He designed a Great Clock with two faces. The clock face outside the house had only an hour hand. A gong sounded every hour. This helped people outside keep track of time. The clock face in the entrance hall measured hours, minutes, and seconds. The inside clock had a pulley and weight system that powered the clock. This clock also showed the day of the week.

Another of Jefferson's designs was a "turning machine" that held his clothes on racks. This made them easy to get to. He even designed a system for opening his parlor doors. When he pulled one door open, the other opened at the same rate.

The Great Clock hung in the great hall of Thomas Jefferson's home for many years.

Jefferson invented a device to make copies of his writing.

Today, these designs don't seem all that special. In Jefferson's time, though, visitors to Monticello found them amazing. His writing desk wasn't so amazing. But he created amazing things on it.

FACT!

As a planter himself, Jefferson always looked for ways to make farming better. He invented a new type of plow. The plow's design made it easier to work in hilly areas.

Jefferson designed items to save time and effort. His writing desk shows this. He wanted it to be easy to use. The desk weighed only 5 pounds (2.3 kilograms). He could carry it with him easily from place to place. The desk was made of mahogany. This beautiful and durable type of wood is often used for furniture. The writing surface was lined with green felt to keep the paper from slipping. The desk measured just under 10 inches (25.4 centimeters) long and 15 inches (38.1 cm) wide. It was just over 3 inches (7.6 cm) deep. It was about the size of a laptop computer today.

Jefferson called his creation a "writing box." It did function as a box. A drawer at one end had space for paper, pen, and an inkwell. The drawer locked. This allowed him to keep things from falling out. The desk also had two leaves with hinges. They folded out to create a writing surface of nearly 20 inches (50.8 cm).

FACT!

The drawer of the writing desk has ink stains in it. They are marks from years of use. It may be that some of the stains came from writing the Declaration of Independence.

The angle of the writing surface on Jefferson's desk could be adjusted to suit the position of the writer.

Once he'd designed the desk, Jefferson needed to have it built. He asked Benjamin Randolph to do the job. Randolph was a well-known furniture maker in Philadelphia. Jefferson had stayed at Randolph's house during earlier visits to the city. Randolph had a reputation for doing fine work. We don't know whether the desk was completed in 1775 or 1776. We do know that Jefferson was pleased with it. We don't know all the papers Jefferson wrote on it. But we do know that he used it to draft the Declaration of Independence.

The desk, when closed, could safely store papers, pens, and other objects.

A writing desk seems like a simple tool. How could it play such an important role in history? Sometimes, an object is simply in the right place at the right time. In someone else's hands, this desk would have been just a desk. But Jefferson was a creative genius, a good writer, and a strong political leader. In 1776, he used the desk to create a document that changed the world.

Benjamin Randolph, Colonial Craftsman

In colonial times, all furniture was made by hand. A skilled craftsperson made each chair, table, or desk one piece at a time. In the 1770s, Benjamin Randolph was among Philadelphia's top furniture makers. He made chairs, bookcases, cabinets, and other objects. He also made special items upon request. One such item was Thomas Jefferson's writing desk. Randolph built the desk using Jefferson's design. That desk became an important part of history.

Benjamin Randolph made lots of furniture. This chair, designed for a famous general in the 1700s, is now in the Metropolitan Museum of Art in New York City.

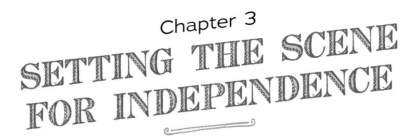

Chapter 3
SETTING THE SCENE FOR INDEPENDENCE

Why is Jefferson's writing desk so well known? Why was the document he wrote so important? For more than 10 years, tension had grown between the 13 colonies and Great Britain. The British government ruled the colonies from more than 3,000 miles (4,828 kilometers) away. Colonists **imported** many common items from Britain. Great Britain taxed some of these goods. A tax is a fee that a government places on something. For example, Britain taxed glass, paper, and tea.

British troops patrolled Fort Hill in Boston Harbor.

British leaders believed these taxes were needed. France and Great Britain had both claimed vast areas of land in America beyond where colonists lived. Between 1754 and 1763, the two nations battled over these lands. British soldiers and colonists fought on one side. French soldiers and American Indians fought on the other. After years of fighting, Britain won the war. The war cost a lot of money. Plus, some British troops remained in the colonies. They stayed to guard the lands Britain had gained. And they had to be fed and housed. British leaders believed the colonies should help pay for these costs. To the British, this seemed fair.

FACT!

Many American Indians were angry that the colonists kept stealing their lands, forcing them to move. The French promised to protect these lands. As a result, many Native nations helped the French. Because of this, the war is often called the French and Indian War.

Many colonists did not agree. They saw themselves as loyal British subjects. But they wanted a say in controlling their own land and running their own government. They already paid taxes to their local colonial governments. They did not think Parliament had the power to tax them since the colonies did not have representatives in the British Parliament.

And the British troops in the colonies weren't just sent for protection. They policed the colonists and even took over their court proceedings.

The British Parliament and king made laws for the Great Britain and the colonies.

Colonists were also angry for another reason. They weren't allowed to take possession of the newly gained lands. Britain wanted to keep peace with the American Indians who lived there. But the colonists thought they should be able to take over American Indian land wherever they wanted. They didn't want Britain telling them where they could live, even though that meant stealing land from Native nations.

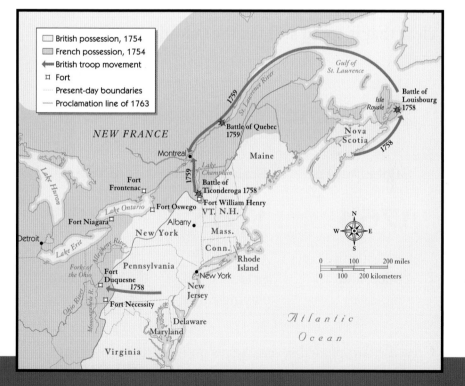

Colonists were not allowed to take possession of land west of what Great Britain called the Proclamation Line of 1763.

In 1764, the British Parliament passed the Sugar Act. This law taxed sugar, coffee, and other items. In 1765, Great Britain added a Stamp Act. This act taxed paper products. The colonists protested. They thought it was unfair for Britain to tax them. The colonists said there should be "no taxation without **representation**." No one represented them in Parliament. They wanted to have a voice about laws and taxes that affected them. In 1766, Parliament dropped the Stamp Act. For a while, tensions eased. However, Parliament made it clear that it could still tax the colonies at any time.

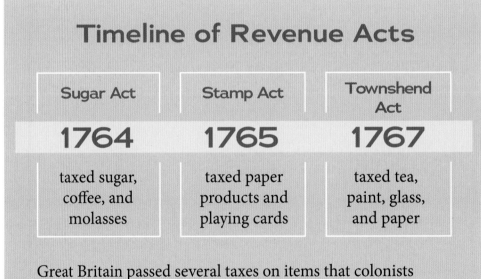

Timeline of Revenue Acts

Sugar Act	Stamp Act	Townshend Act
1764	**1765**	**1767**
taxed sugar, coffee, and molasses	taxed paper products and playing cards	taxed tea, paint, glass, and paper

Great Britain passed several taxes on items that colonists imported. These taxes angered colonists and helped lead to the Revolutionary War.

Then in 1767, Parliament passed the Townshend Act. This law taxed tea, paint, glass, and paper imported from Great Britain. The British sent troops to make sure colonists paid the new taxes. Colonists did not want British soldiers with guns policing them. They protested by **boycotting** these British products. By 1770, hostilities reached an all-time high.

After the colonists protested the new taxes, the British sent more troops to enforce the law.

Many of the loudest protests took place in Boston, Massachusetts. To maintain control, Britain sent additional troops there in 1768. Tensions between colonists and the British troops grew. On March 5, 1770, an angry mob shouted insults at British soldiers. The soldiers fired shots into the crowd. Five colonists were killed at British hands. This action became known as the Boston Massacre. It made people throughout the colonies see the British as enemies.

The Boston Massacre did more than anything else to raise the call for revolution.

In April 1770, Britain dropped almost all the taxes. They kept just one—on tea. Colonists hated this tax most of all. Almost everyone drank tea. In December 1773, colonists climbed aboard British ships in Boston Harbor. They dumped 342 chests of tea the ships were carrying into the water. The event became known as the Boston Tea Party. Parliament then decided to punish the people of Boston. The British closed the city's harbor. They brought more troops into the city. Anger against Britain reached new heights.

Uniting the Colonies

Until the 1770s, each colony looked out for itself. There was little cooperation among them. That changed after the Boston Tea Party. Britain's harsh response united the colonies against Britain. They banded together to fight the Revolutionary War.

Patriotic colonists met to plan boycotts and other protests against what they deemed Great Britain's unfair rule.

Tensions with Britain grew worse and worse. In September 1774, delegates from 12 of the 13 colonies met in Philadelphia. This First Continental Congress discussed what actions to take. Congress still hoped to solve the problems with Britain peacefully. Then, in April 1775, armed fighting began. British troops clashed with colonial **militia** in Lexington and Concord, Massachusetts. The Revolutionary War had begun.

When the Second Continental Congress met, they chose George Washington to be commander-in-chief of the army.

The Second Continental Congress first met in May 1775. Colonial leaders formed an army. They chose George Washington as its leader. Fighting continued throughout the year. Still, both sides hoped to avoid a long, full-scale war. In July 1775, Congress made a final effort to bring peace. Congress sent a letter to King George III. This letter asked for better treatment of the colonies. The king wouldn't read it. Instead, he declared that the colonies were in a state of **rebellion**. He prepared to send more British troops to America.

> ### FACT!
> The battles between colonial militia and British troops at Lexington and Concord were minor fights. But they marked the first battles of the Revolutionary War. The first gunshot at Concord became known as "the shot heard 'round the world."

In early 1776, some colonists still supported Britain. Others believed the colonies should break away and form a new nation. By June, Congress was ready to vote on independence. No one knew if all the colonies would support this move. Congress wanted to be prepared. If delegates voted for independence, Congress wanted to have a document stating the reasons. Congress formed a committee to work on the document. Jefferson was asked to draft it.

Thomas Jefferson was chosen to draft the colonists' document on independence because he was a respected member of the group—and an excellent writer.

Breaking ties with Britain was dangerous. The British government would view such an act as **treason**. The leaders of the independence movement could face death. Britain had the world's strongest army and navy. The colonists' army was weak. They had no navy. Also, many colonists were still unsure about breaking ties with Britain. That was a second reason for Jefferson's document. Congress wanted colonists to unite for independence. This paper would explain why such a drastic step was needed.

Common Sense

In January 1776, a colonist named Thomas Paine published a pamphlet. He titled it *Common Sense*. Paine wrote that being ruled by a king made no sense. He said that people should have a role in creating a nation's laws. The colonists did not have this role under British rule. He urged the colonists to break away from Britain. Then they could form their own government. Paine's pamphlet was a best seller. It convinced many people to support the independence movement.

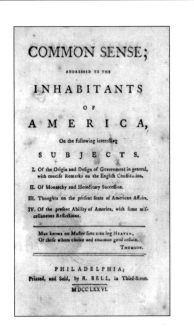

Common Sense became a runaway best seller. It is still in print today.

Chapter 4
DECLARING INDEPENDENCE

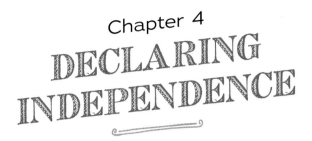

Jefferson seemed to be a perfect choice to draft this paper. The members of Congress knew he wrote well. After the first battles of the war in 1775, he had helped Congress draft a statement. That statement explained why the colonists felt they needed to fight for their rights. He also had helped Virginia prepare a paper calling for independence. He had just drafted a **constitution** for Virginia. He could use some of these same ideas now.

Jefferson wrote the draft of the Declaration of Independence at Graff House in Philadelphia.

Jefferson was one of five delegates charged with preparing this document. Congress appointed the delegates on June 11, 1776. The committee discussed key points the document should make. Then Jefferson got to work. At the time, he thought preparing for the independence vote was the most important work of Congress. This document was just a small part of it. Still, he dove headfirst into the project. His location at Graff House was perfect. It was just a few minutes from where Congress met. Jefferson could quickly move from attending meetings to writing.

FACT!

The five delegates working on the document were Thomas Jefferson, John Adams, Benjamin Franklin, Robert Livingston, and Roger Sherman. Jefferson was viewed as the best writer in the group. He was asked to prepare the draft for the others to review.

Jefferson probably did his writing in the parlor of his rented rooms. His writing desk served him well. Jefferson stood 6 feet, 2 inches (187.9 cm) tall. That was quite tall for those times. The desk's slanted surface brought the paper closer to him. Sometimes, he worked early in the morning before Congress began its meetings. Other times, he worked at night by candlelight. Word by word, he crafted the document. Some drafts of the paper survive. We know from these drafts that Jefferson edited his work carefully. He made many changes along the way.

Painter John Trumbull created a famous painting of Jefferson presenting the Declaration of Independence to Congress.

Jefferson (right) showed a draft of the Declaration to Benjamin Franklin (left) and John Adams (center).

No one knows exactly how long Jefferson spent writing his draft. Most experts believe it took about two weeks. Jefferson showed a draft to John Adams and Benjamin Franklin in late June. They made only a few minor changes. Jefferson approved these changes. On June 28, Jefferson read the document to the full Congress.

FACT!

A famous painting by John Trumbull called *Declaration of Independence* shows Jefferson presenting the document to Congress. For years, people thought the painting showed the document's passage on July 4. Instead, the painting shows its introduction on June 28.

Jefferson's paper began with a statement of purpose. It was meant to "declare the causes" that led the colonies to break away from Britain. The second paragraph is the most famous. It describes people's rights to "Life, Liberty, and the pursuit of Happiness." These words were meant to inspire the colonists.

Next, Jefferson listed a series of complaints against King George III. Jefferson accused the king of being a **tyrant**. He wrote that the king had abused the rights of the colonists.

This rough draft of the Declaration of Independence shows how Thomas Jefferson edited his writing.

The king had cut off their trade with the rest of the world. The king had taxed them without their consent. He had placed British troops in the colonies. The list includes more than 25 complaints. The document closed by saying that the united colonies were now "Free and Independent" states. At the end, the document's signers made

Most of Jefferson's complaints against King George III did not make it into the final version of the Declaration.

a pledge to stick together. They pledged "our Lives, our Fortunes and our sacred Honor."

FACT!

Today, we know this famous document as the Declaration of Independence. That wasn't its name at first. In 1776, it was published as "A Declaration by the Representatives of the United States of America."

Congress did not discuss Jefferson's document right away. First, it debated the motion to declare independence. On July 2, that motion passed. The colonies had declared themselves free of British rule! Then Congress spent two days discussing Jefferson's document. Delegates argued about some of the wording. In all, Congress made more than 80 changes to the document. Nearly 500 words were cut, including some of the complaints Jefferson had made against the king.

Congress got together to debate and make changes to Jefferson's Declaration.

Looking back, most experts agree that the edits made the document better. Jefferson strongly disagreed. Like many writers, he did not like having his words changed. On July 4, Congress approved the revised document. Then they sent it to be printed. The Declaration of Independence was about to become part of history. And so was the desk it was written on.

In July 1776, colonists pulled down the statue of King George III in the Wall Street area of New York City.

FACT!

Members of Congress did not sign the Declaration of Independence on July 4, 1776. The signing took place on August 2.

Members of Congress changed many details in Jefferson's document. They made no changes to its opening two paragraphs. One statement there ranks among the most famous in history:

"We hold these truths to be self-evident, that all men are created equal, that they are endowed by their Creator with certain unalienable rights, that among these are Life, Liberty, and the pursuit of Happiness.—That to secure these rights, Governments are instituted among Men, deriving their just powers from the consent of the governed."

These words said that people had certain basic rights. Governments could not take away these rights. Instead, governments should always do what is best for the people. If they don't, the people should have the right to change the government. The power should rest with the people. At the time, few world governments worked this way. Kings or queens ruled most major countries. The Declaration of Independence laid out a new way for governments to work.

After the Declaration was approved, it was read out to the public at many sites. Among them were the steps of the Pennsylvania State House, later known as Independence Hall.

"All Men Are Created Equal"

The Declaration of Independence said "all men are created equal." It left out women. Women still had few rights. It also left out American Indians and Black men, both enslaved and free. It would take nearly 100 years until those who

Women, Black people, and American Indians were not considered equal in America at the time of the Declaration.

had been enslaved in America became free. In fact, in the 1770s, only white men who owned property could vote. Today, American laws apply to all people equally.

Chapter 5

A LONG LIFE FOR THE WRITING DESK

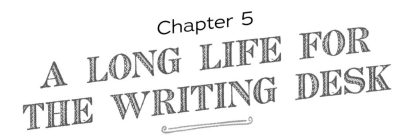

The story of Jefferson's writing desk was just beginning in 1776. He used the desk for nearly 50 years. He used it from 1801 to 1809 while he was president of the United States. In 1803, he engineered and approved the Louisiana Purchase. This purchase doubled the size of the young United States. He may have used the desk to write letters about the purchase. He may have used it to approve the journey of Meriwether Lewis and William Clark. In 1804, they began a two-year journey to explore the new lands that were now part of the United States.

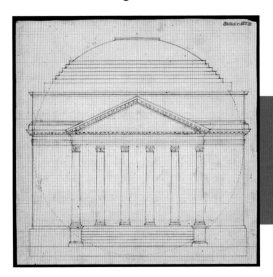

Jefferson may have drawn up the plans for the University of Virginia on his writing desk.

The Louisiana Purchase

Total Size: 828,000 square miles (2,144,510 square km)

Total Cost: $15 million

Cost per Acre: about 3 cents

States Involved: 15 states were formed or added to as a result of the Louisiana Purchase

After two terms as president, Jefferson returned to Monticello. There, he began plans to form a university. The University of Virginia opened in 1819. Jefferson designed how the campus would look. He planned many of its buildings. Jefferson may have used his writing desk as he drew up these plans. Today, the University of Virginia still ranks among the nation's top public universities.

Jefferson knew his writing desk had a place in history. He wanted it to remain in his family. In 1825, he gave it as a wedding present to his granddaughter, Ellen Randolph. At first, he planned to give her a different gift. He had the cabinetmaker at Monticello build a desk for her. The ship carrying the desk to her in Boston sank at sea. Jefferson then decided to give her his own writing desk instead.

Jefferson's home of Monticello is now a tourist attraction. Visitors can see what life was like in Jefferson's time.

Jefferson described his desk as "plain, neat, convenient." He noted that it took up little space. He told Ellen that the desk's value "will increase with the years." He knew it would always be linked with the Declaration of Independence.

The desk remained in the family until 1880. Then the family gave it to the U.S. government. The Smithsonian Institution has had the desk since 1921. Visitors can see it on display at the National Museum of American History.

FACT!

Thomas Jefferson died on July 4, 1826. That was exactly 50 years after the Declaration of Independence was approved. John Adams, another member of the committee, and the second president of the new nation, died that same day.

Chapter 6
LASTING LEGACY

Nearly 250 years have passed since Thomas Jefferson wrote the Declaration of Independence. Even today, it remains a symbol of freedom. It reminds us of our nation's struggle to break away from British rule. It reminds us of the ideals upon which the United States was founded. The Declaration's importance extends worldwide. Over the years, many other nations have turned to it. Its messages of freedom and equal rights have inspired others to seek their own freedom. Today, more than half the world's countries have a similar document.

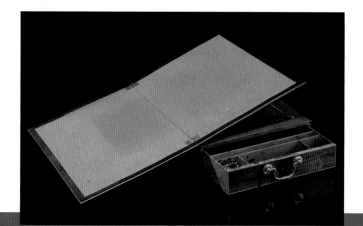

Jefferson's desk is a reminder—an artifact—of the successful fight for freedom by the American colonies.

The opening words of the Declaration of Independence are carved on the wall of the Thomas Jefferson Memorial.

And it all began on a simple wooden desk. The desk itself serves as a symbol. It shows the creativity of our third president, who designed it. Then he used it to create a document that changed the world.

The Assembly Room at Independence Hall

Independence Hall

Other objects also remind us of what happened in 1776. For instance, visitors to Philadelphia can tour the building where the Continental Congress met. It is now known as Independence Hall. Visitors can see the room where the Declaration of Independence was signed. They can imagine the excitement when the document was approved.

Syng Inkstand

Syng Inkstand

Visitors to Independence Hall can also see other objects related to the Declaration of Independence. For instance, they can see a silver inkstand made by Philip Syng. Delegates used this inkstand when they signed the document.

Liberty Bell

The Liberty Bell is also nearby. It serves as another symbol of freedom. Surprisingly, the bell did not ring when the document was signed.

Graff House

The Graff House, where Jefferson did his writing, is just a few blocks away. All of these landmarks in Center City, Philadelphia, bring history to life.

GLOSSARY

artifact (AHR-tuh-fakt)—an object that plays an important role in history

boycott (BOI-kot)—to refuse to buy certain products

constitution (kon-sti-TOO-shuhn)—the system of rules and laws under which a group is governed

declaration (dek-luh-RAY-shuhn)—formal statement

delegate (DE-li-get)—a person sent to represent others at a meeting or event

imported (im-POHRT-ed)—coming into one country from another country

militia (mi-LISH-uh)—a military force made up of civilians, created to serve in emergencies

Parliament (PAHR-luh-muhnt)—the highest lawmaking body in Great Britain

rebellion (ri-BEL-yuhn)—the act of resisting a government or ruler

representation (rep-ri-zen-TAY-shuhn)—having someone stand up for your interests in government

subject (SUHB-jikt)—someone who is ruled by a person or government

treason (TREE-zuhn)—betraying one's country

tyrant (TIE-ruhnt)—a cruel or unjust ruler

unalienable (uhn-AYL-yuh-nuh-buhl)—not able to be taken away

READ MORE

Adler, David A. *A Picture Book of Thomas Jefferson*. New York: Holiday House, 2018.

Clay, Kathryn. *The Declaration of Independence: Introducing Primary Sources*. North Mankato, MN: Capstone Press, 2018.

Murray, Laura K. *The Declaration of Independence*. North Mankato, MN: Capstone Press, 2020.

INTERNET SITES

Ben's Guide to the U.S. Government: The Declaration of Independence
bensguide.gpo.gov/declaration-of-independence-1776

Biography: President Thomas Jefferson
ducksters.com/biography/uspresidents/thomasjefferson.php

Monticello Facts for Kids
kids.kiddle.co/Monticello

The Declaration of Independence: What Does it Say?
archives.gov/founding-docs/declaration/what-does-it-say

INDEX